MY LIFE IS YOUR LIFE.
YOUR LIFE IS MY LIFE.

By Julio Flores

TABLE OF CONTENTS

Intro

This book reveals my life story from beginning of my childhood to present day. I wrote this book because I believe that our youth who face adversities everyday have the power to transform their lives

This book will help you understand my journey and how I made it out of the invisible boxes that I could only see and in some cases I couldn't see. The invisible box stands for any issues or habits/ways that I was living. After experiencing many different issues, I was able to turn all my struggles into my strengths and accomplish the unbelievable. I was able to find my way out of my many invisible boxes.

This book is written to speak to a young adult audience, for those young people who have given up on themselves, who have lost hope. I truly believe we have to believe in them so much, that we need to show them how to believe in themselves. I hope you enjoy this book, and it will inspire you to believe that you also can get out of any invisible box you might be stuck in. My goal is for everyone that will read this book, will be inspired to take charge of their choices and lives. Adults will complement this process by opening more doors of opportunity to these at promise young adults.

I can remember as far back as a young boy, moving to Denver from Puerto Rico, only knowing Spanish and having to learn English. Remembering the first time I saw snow and going to school for the first time. I do remember kids being mean to me, making fun of me on how I spoke, after going through some rough times I started to meet friends.

I hope we can come together to provide young people the tools for overcoming the many adversities that they encounter in our society.

"I believe we need to build a legacy of relationships that last a lifetime." -Anonymous

The Journey

My name is Julius Rosario Flores (Julio), born in Pennsylvania, Philadelphia. Maria Flores is my mother's name and I have never met my biological father. My stepdad helped raised me until I was about 12 years old. After being born we lived in a small apartment in Pennsylvania for about a year.

I remember my mom would tell me how she had to fight away the rats that were trying to get to me, she would do everything she could to keep them from reaching me. After a while there we moved on and my mother moved us to Puerto Rico. Arecibo, San Juan, Puerto Rico, this is where I was raised until I was 8 years old.

I have some memories of our house, the school I went to, the carnivals that were on the beach, going to the beach with my family, and the road we would travel on to get to San Juan. We would take a small white van that would take us into town. Years later I can still remember the food I grew up eating, like pastelillos, maduros, chuletas and arroz con gandules. Now that I am older, I can't remember any of my family, the celebrations in the neighborhood were so much fun and sometimes scary because of the way they would dress up.

The vejigante is a folkloric figure whose origins trace back to medieval Spain. The legend goes that the vejigante represented the infidel Moors who were defeated in a battle led by Saint James. To honor the saint, the people dressed as demons took to the street in an annual procession. Over time, the vejigante became a kind of folkloric demon, but in Puerto Rico, it took on a new dimension with the introduction of African and native Taíno cultural influence.

Being so young I could only remember so much and to be honest I did not understand what they were celebrating. People would get together and march down the streets and they would celebrate together as a community. I remember my mom cooking for a lot of people, during the time they were at the house, I was so freaked out because they looked evil. The waterfalls that

I can remember, going with my stepdad fishing and watching him catch a lot of fish with a large net.

The sugar canes that he would collect for us were the best, I would spend hours biting and chewing off all the sweetness of the stick. I was too young to really do anything but I loved playing in the water. The ocean will always be a part of my life.

Then we were moving on at age 8, 1981. I started to wonder what is going on? Why are we leaving Puerto Rico, where are we going, and wow look at the Ocean it's huge!! I remember flying into Denver, it was the first time I ever saw snow, it was cold and I remember the Denny's on Federal. It is where we first stopped to eat when we arrived in Denver, I was scared because I did not know what the people were saying.

They were all speaking in English and I did not know any of these people. We were now living in Denver, I was meeting new family members, started going to school at Brown Elementary while living in a small apartment in the north side of Denver. One thing I will always remember is being bullied in school because I was different. I didn't know much English and being in elementary school the kids were mean, I tried so hard to speak English and learn words as fast as I could and yet they would still make fun of me. They would make fun of how I would pronounce words, then after dealing with the bullies for a while I started to be mean also.

I would say hurtful things and fight back all the time, then after some time I started to make friends that accepted me for who I was and still till this day I know some of my friends I made in elementary school.

I have a cousin her name is Susie and she was older than me, when I first got here I spoke Spanish all the time. I knew a little bit of English but not enough, so cousin Susie would always tell me not to speak to her unless it was English. I really enjoyed being around my cousin so I started to learn English really quick.

I look back to all the people like my cousin and all those that were giving me a hard time about not knowing English. I would like to thank them all now because I was no longer afraid, they helped me step out of my invisible box.

My Mother

My mother Maria is a tough woman, she has always been there for me and my sister. I can remember when I was a young kid, I always loved being around my mother, she would make fresh tortillas, she would have me clean out the beans and I loved when she baked cakes because I would eat the frosting after she was done.

My mother would work all the time then she would like to go out, I remember she would love to dance and drink. At our house we always had company, mom would always have plenty of food for everyone. As years went by, she started to have bad feelings about my stepdad and then not too long after, she found out that he was cheating on her.

I remember when they would fight, and I would sit and just watch. I will always remember this one day when my mom and stepdad were arguing, she took bags of weed and she started to throw it all over the place in the living room.

I was sitting down watching them, after arguing for about 20 minutes at the door you could hear the Police knocking. As they were knocking at the door my mom and stepdad started to pick up the weed, stuffing the weed into the couch, under the couch and after they opened the door the officer started talking to them, then after the officer left nothing happened. So, my mom and stepdad moved on living in that invisible box that I could only see, my mom knew something was not right after awhile she took the steps to get out of her invisible box, she then got out left my stepdad, and she started her new life.

I know it was not easy for her, but she worked hard, she always did her best to have food for my sister and me. I am so happy that my mom had the courage and strength to step out of her invisible box. Remember we all have plenty of invisible boxes that we carry with us.

Okay now my mom did not have my stepdad around, she did not have much money, so we lived off food stamps, my mom would do anything she could do to get us food. We did have nights when we did not have much to eat, but my mom taught

us how to survive on beans, oatmeal, cereal, tortillas,

I think you get it.

See it is easy for people to say what they want or assume that they

know what we are going through. Hunger is real. It affects your

mental status, and I believe I was acting out sometimes because

of hunger. I also believe because I was not eating well that it

caused me to fall behind academically.

Years went by and my mom started to get things together, she

showed my sister and me how to stay strong, she showed me that

no matter what situation is brought to you that there is an answer,

not to ever give up and do what you need to do to survive.

So, I did all this, throughout my life I learned how to do things in

the right way, my invisible boxes were coming to an end.

Thank you, mom, for not ever giving up on your kids.

After getting her life together and meeting my stepdad Fabian, she started to get things right, she was starting to feel good about life. My sister Tammy was the baby, she was growing up fast. Growing up with my family moving from place to place, having to start over every time in a new neighborhood, having to make new friends was not always fun, to be honest it never really was fun.

Seeing my mom have to start over with her relationship with my stepdad Fabian was hard, as they were getting to know each other they also had a lot of invisible boxes that they were trying to get out of. They had to learn to understand each other, they would drink sometimes and get into arguments. As I became a teen, I got much stronger plus I ended up picking up a very bad temper/attitude, I do remember trying to protect my mother when they would fight. It did not work much because their love was so strong that both of them were blind to their own invisible boxes.

Years had gone by when they both started to work on their own invisible boxes, then after they both started to balance their life, yes getting older had to do with them having to change their life. I am so happy that they did, cause now we have all grown up, my sister and I have our own kids that are now all grown up.

When my mom became a grandmother to mine and my sisters kids, I believe that helped her change her ways, she has been there for all of them. Now she is a great grandmother to my grandson plus my sister's grandkids. Mom thanks for always being available when we all needed you, Love You.

The Separation the Truth

Shortly after my mother and my first stepdad separated, my mother broke the news that my father was not who I thought he was. For most of my life, till I was about twelve I always thought he was my biological father, well after they separated, I was told the truth. To be honest I was not that mad, for most of my life I always felt that I was a stepchild to him, he would buy my sister all the nice stuff, she always got what she wanted. I just got what was given to me by my mother, maybe my stepdad tried to love me, I just don't know because that is how things were when I was young.

I had a stepdad that sold drugs, who was out cheating on my mother, and man, this was really a huge turning point in my life. When he cheated on my mother I had to see her go through the pain of finding out that he was with another woman, on top of all that he was abusive to my mother, this is what made me change the way I was.

My mom was a mess and she had her own thing going on. I started to run the streets, I would find ways to get what I wanted, plus live the way I wanted because my mother was always working, even though she had other things going on she was so good to my sister and me.

I can say that my mother was always there for me until she started feeling the pain of her heart being broken, before my mother got separated she was always looking so beautiful, as a kid I always thought she was the only woman that I would ever love. No matter how I felt about the way my stepdad treated me, she always made sure I was taken care of.

After the breakup she started going out, meeting new men, this is When I started to have more time for myself, this is when I started to hit the streets. I would be at my friends' houses or at the Boys Club. My mother would sometimes be in her own world, she would drink, go dancing and hang out with her friends.
I have to say that during this time when my mother was doing her own thing, trying to find her way back to the happy woman

that she was. I never stopped loving her, I never had hate for her, I just kept going. I do wish she would have been able to come to more of my games, when I played football, basketball and baseball.

I was really good at all 3 sports and it was really bad enough that I had no father there for me, so it would have helped me if she would have been there. It is okay, now I get it she had a lot going on and she had to work in order to take care of my sister and me.

There would be days where she did not have much for us, Sometimes we just had oatmeal with bread in it just to help fill us up. If we did not have oatmeal there were days where we had cereal but no milk, so she would have the powder that we would mix with water to replace the milk sometimes it tasted like water but if you added a lot of sugar it was good. I remember when she would make homemade tortillas. I would watch her and wait for her to start rolling the tortilla, after a few of them were done I would eat them while they were still hot and fresh. She is the best cook ever, no matter what she made it was yummy. Another thing that I would love to do is separate the bad beans, she would spread the beans on the dinner table so I could pick out the bad ones. As time went on things got better and my mother found love again, this was when she was able to step out of her invisible box.

Now being young, I was dealing with a lot of changes, I had a bad temper plus a bad attitude, yes everything was starting to get to me all the time. I was getting bullied, parents separating, not having much, my mother hurting, experiencing some abuse in my life, and finding out that my stepdad was not my real father.

After dealing with all these different issues for a while, I began to cut myself. It did not take much to make me mad or sad, so when people did I would go find a knife or anything that was sharp, I would take it and for some reason I would just start cutting my left arm. Afterwards I would have marks and scabs all over. Not too many people would ask why my arm was marked up and those that would, I always had some kind of answer that worked for me.

Now growing up with a bad temper I had lots of issues that would come up, but this one cutting myself was one that I was really good at. I also would like to break things like mirrors, putting holes in walls/doors, or just walking up to a random car to break the window. I was good at making sure that not too many people would find out about my invisible boxes, only a small group of people knew anything about my pain, I had a few friends that knew about my actions, then my mother learned more about me as I grew up. Not too many of my family members even knew I was stuck in my invisible boxes.

Now we started over in a new apartment, duplexes and smaller homes, now growing up in the hood, most places we moved in had roaches, every once in a while, we would have to leave our place so that way they could spray/bomb our home to help control the roaches. After a while this was a norm everyone that lived by us was going through this, you can say roaches were apart of the family. After years of dealing with this lifestyle my mom finally got us away from living with roaches.

Why do I bring this up because many of our youth are dealing with this type of lifestyle. I want them to know that they are not alone, many folks are dealing with this, many would not write about this, but I am. It is important that those that are reading this book, know that they can step out of that invisible box that many people don't want them to do. Enough is enough we all are equal, we can do anything we believe in, I have proven this, once again, as I did not graduate from high school and never got a G.E.D.

I have become a great citizen and leader/mentor, I have become a successful man and a great Director for the Boys & Girls Club. I am a great father, husband, brother, grandfather plus a father/brother figure to hundreds of young people.

The Letdown

Now mom had to enroll me in school. First day of school at Brown Elementary was not something I really remember, I do remember that kids always made fun of me when I would try to speak English, they would laugh at me. In time, I learned to speak more English and I started to stand up for myself, then I started to have more friends.

Time to move on to Colfax Elementary new chapter, new friends. This was the school where I started learning to fight back, this is when I started to get in trouble for standing up for myself. I knew it was wrong but no one was doing anything about it, teachers were not trying to help me, they were trying to teach me how to speak and pronounce words correctly.
I just could not get away from trouble, now it's time to move on to Lake Middle School.

Now the fights continued but they never did get easier. I still did not care for many people at the school, but I was able to make a few more friends. I was always questioning myself on why I wanted to go back to school because every time I was there the teachers and principal would treat me like I did not belong there. Suspensions began and this is when I started to miss more days of school, I learned really quick how easy it was to stay home from school.

Now high school is here, North High School and of course I was now on track on missing days, on any given day I would just stay home or go to school for a few hours and then just leave. I felt that no one really cared, I tried to fit in and for most people they really thought I was a good person and I was but I happen to be surrounded by teachers that did not want to take on a teen that did not give much effort to come to school.

So, the fights continued, and issues just kept coming, then I was transferred to my second-high school. West High and it was the same, so then I was transferred to my third high school Lincoln High this is where I felt more welcomed and yes there were a few teachers that tried to help me out but at this time I was too deep into the streets and it just did not work out. I was stuck in my invisible box and it became who I was at that time in my life.

The streets had a hold on me this is when I started believing what the streets had to offer. The weekends would come around and we would party all the time. This is where I would find myself running into people that did not like me. In my teens years, I have been shot at multiple times, I had got into plenty of fights at parties, I remember a few times when being at a few house parties and then they both got shot up, everyone in the house was scared.

It got to the point that my mom had moved us to Leadville, Colorado up in the mountains. This is where I started my 4th high school and for the most part I was doing good. I played basketball for the JV team, I also played baseball, I had a lot of friends and my cousins took care of me. We were having parties during the weekends or going to parties, things were looking up for me.

Not to long after all this I got with a few people and we decided to break into a house where we took a Nintendo a VCR plus some other items, we kept them at my place, after about a week I had the police at my door, someone that I did the crime with turned me in, I ended up taking the charge by myself. I got 4 years of probation and I returned everything back to the owner of the house. Here we go again, my mother moved us back to the city where we moved to Littleton Colorado. Yes, for the 2 years I had to report to my probation officer in Leadville after my mom was able to get my case transferred to Denver, then we tried one more time I went back to Lincoln High School after a while I just could not escape my invisible boxes, I just did not have enough support from family or anyone, so I decided to drop out of high school.

I started to work, driving a bobcat working construction for about 4 years. I was working 6 days a week from morning to night, I still remember how hard it was that sometimes I would fall asleep at work, I did whatever I needed to do, washing streets, and picking up trash at construction sites. Working for Frank really helped me learn about being responsible, Frank was always there for me. I remember one time I ran the tractor into a classic Chevy Nova when I was grading the lot of a brand-new home, Frank paid for it up front, to save me from getting a ticket.

During this time, I was dating and already had a daughter, being young and not knowing much about relationships and how to raise a daughter things were not going well for me. One day the person that I was dating had made me upset. I spoke to her on the pay phone next to V's Liquor store here in Denver, after hanging up the phone I was very upset I decided to pick up a large rock I then threw it at the window of the liquor store, it was a Sunday, so it was closed, it was night time.

After it broke, I was so upset that I waited for the police to come and after so many minutes later no one came so I decided to grab items from the liquor store. I took them back to my apartment, as I was doing this some of my friends saw that I was bringing liquor home so they joined in and started to take items themselves. A few days had gone by I thought I had got away with this, so I relaxed and did not worry about it anymore. I remember I got really sick and got strep throat, so my mom took me to the doctors, after we got home the apartment was hit hard by the police. They had left a paper on the dinner table with a list of items that were taken from the apartment, also I had to turn myself in, we get to the police station, they start asking me how it all went down. I told them after they were done speaking to me they arrested me, I got out on bail then after court I got another 4 years of probation, after 2 years I was let off probation for good behavior.

Back in the late 80's and early 90's school was not like how it is today, teachers did not teach to the heart, also after school programs were not focusing on academics they were too busy trying to get us to stop being violent and trying to keep us alive

and off the streets. I was all over the place and did what I

wanted, what I really needed was someone to guide me,

to show me the way out of my invisible boxes.

I was always a hard worker and for the most part pretty smart.

Most people during my youth years may have been trying to

guide me, the sad thing is I can say only a few teachers cared. I

let myself down by thinking others cared about me. I let myself

down by thinking the school system let me down, the truth is we

all have control over our choices, yes, it is nice to have people

there for you but at the end of the day you are the one that has

to be there for yourself.

Don't be in denial dig deep, have the strength to step out of

your invisible box. Be the change you wish to see in others,

lead by example and be as successful as you wish to be.

The day I choose to drop out of high school, I started to work

and I became a hard worker with the help of great people that supported me along the way. After many years of learning, I decided to continue to move up with my jobs, with no education, I have managed to become a hard worker, a caring person that is able to help others. I managed in construction for many years, I then stepped out of my invisible box and started a new journey in retail, I worked in many different departments, I then moved up to management and worked in retail for 16 years, then I started giving back to my community, I became a volunteer at the Boys & Girls Club.

All this helped me stay out of my invisible box it showed me how to help others, I now have a great job where I can help others believe in themselves.

For those that are reading this keep in mind we all have our own path and it's up to you to make that choice on which one you want to take. Most important make sure to step out of your invisible boxes don't be a victim of your own circumstances.

The Streets/ The Hood

By the time I was 13 years old I was running the streets, I felt like a man or at least I thought I was a man at that age. When you grow up in the hood you have to adapt to fit in, you have to learn to walk sometimes or even when to run.

Seeing the easy route is a huge part of the streets, what I mean by that is, when I was 13 years old the streets got a hold of me, it started to show me all the easy things to do. I would steal from others, I would break into cars and sell any items I could get my hands on. I stopped going to school all the time because it was easy to just hang out with my friends, I would spend the night at my friends or anyone's house that was cool with me staying there.

My mom was always working or going out, so I was able to come home or stay where ever I wanted, my mother always thought I was a good kid. Then I started to get into trouble with the law, which then made me a juvenile.

They would always contact my mom and that is when she started to see that I was getting into trouble and hanging out with the wrong type of crowds.

I have always told people that I was never involved in gangs but that I was a hood gangster, I was always getting into a fight, getting sweated by someone on the streets. I had so many friends that were in different gangs, they were all cool with me because they knew I was not involved in any gangs, they also knew I was crazy and had their back.

When I was about 14 years old myself plus some of my friends started a group called Everlasting Crew, we did this because we loved to dance and party all the time. After a while we started a second crew called Love Crew before you knew it, we were about 30 deep. So when the weekends would come we would all roll together, go to parties, some of us had our Everlasting Crew shirts on and some had our Love Crew shirts on.

Mike, Tony, Mario, Carlos, Compton R.I.P, plus a few more friends we were always together, boy do I miss being with my friends. We would jam out with music all the time, I remember when we would do food and gas runs. Man, time has change you really can't do that anymore, well maybe food runs.

Now you're probably thinking wow what type of life were you living, well all this was normal for many of us that grew up in the hood. See for kids that grow up in this type of environment we all learn from each other, we learn this from going to school with each other or at the Boys Club back in the days before it became Boys & Girls Club. See this type of behavior came to us in the hood like the style of clothing, we all pay attention to what others were wearing it's the same thing with habits of how we act plus talk in our community.

Now with all this attention we were always being challenged by someone, we all had each other's backs, yes, we would get into our share of fights. My boy Mario aka Beiner was crazy he always had my back, Compton was down he was killed over a debt owed over drugs, Mike aka Bumpers was the coolest he always had plenty of hairspray on the side of his hair when he had his hats on, he always had my back always, he was not always the best fighter, but he somehow would be there for me no matter what went down. My boy Carlos aka Gargamel was always ready to dance, last my boy Tony aka Lurch he was the one out of all my good friends that loved to party, he would drink and chill he also loved to play ball, he was amazing at playing basketball.

See the streets make everything feel right and easy so with that I was hooked. After getting tickets all the time from the police plus always getting pulled over because I had a hoodie on or a hat. I remember when the officer that drove around my hood would pull us over walking or driving, he would have a picture of you he kept it in his car, it was his way to track us down, so when we would have any warrants, he would have your name, picture plus he knew where you lived so he would come visit you or he would look for you in the neighborhood.

Now I drove all the time when I was a teenager without a license so I was already setting myself up for failure. I would drive around my mother's yellow Datsun sunny 1200 4 door, I took that car and added a Kenwood stereo with 25-inch speakers and a 2000-watt amp yes the car was booming. I then added some stickers on the front windshield that said "Cold Chilling", now we were ready to cruise on 38th ave, on Federal Blvd.

Sometimes we would cruise all night find places to go to, it did not matter. I remember one time my mom was in the car we could hear her coming from a couple of blocks away she had her Spanish music blasting it was crazy to see her pull up in the car all my friends loved it. My mother was the coolest mother anyone could have, but it did not do me any favors because I took advantage of her, that is why I was able to hit the streets all the time.

Now I could have sold drugs, for a while I ran drugs from Denver to Colorado Springs. Yes, I made easy money cause that's what the streets do for you to get you hooked, but I was not feeling it after doing this, I was scared that I would get caught, it started to remind me of my stepdad that sold drugs and cheated on my mom. I did not want to turn out like him so I gave that up real quick.

After years of running the streets I turned 15, the streets plus the hood really took me to a dark place, I started to drink and smoke weed. One night after drinking so much, I was taken to the hospital. I was throwing up all over the place, I remember that my friends that took me to the hospital and had a plastic bag full of my throw up. I was 4 times the limit and had alcohol poisoning, this was on a Friday, I remember having my hangover on that Sunday. I thought I was going to die that weekend.

Growing up in the hood I saw my share of deaths, I remember losing a friend who was killed execution style, all because his mother owed money to her drug dealer, that really hurt all my friends, we all moved on continued our life's surviving the hood. After all this I went on living life, I was always fighting looking for a reason to fight, I would go to parties if you looked at me, I would say something, my friends would always have to stop me from doing or saying something.

There was a time when we were at a party, the apartment was full and I was talking to a girl who now is my wife of 27 years. We were at this party, things were not going good for me so she was not wanting to be with me at the time. I called my friends into the bathroom and asked all of them if they were down, they were looking at me like no don't do this Julio, I repeated to them this is your chance to show me that your down, I told them when I get out of this bathroom, I am going to go out there and start some shit, this is the time for you to show me that you are down.

So, I did, things got crazy, some of the gangster that were there were my friends from growing up in the hood. When I said fuck all you it got real quiet, everyone just stood looking at me after a few seconds boom everyone started to say something back to me and my friends. As I made my way to the front door I was just outside and some guy came at me, I pulled my butterfly knife out went right at him with it, my good friend Mario took it away from me while he was doing that, he cut his hand really good. At this point we were outnumbered, so we made our way to the car, started to get in the car, some big dude comes from who knows where and he started to hit the car, we took off speeding down the street, we then met up with some of our hood friends.

Then as we we're getting Mario's hand cleaned up, we then got some of our friends made our way back to the party that we just left. We had about 20 of us, we surrounded the apartment, we came up on them real quiet they had no idea we were coming, boom that big dude saw us then we started to break windows, rocks were going into the apartment then we took off back to my boys house a few blocks away, as we were just getting back to his house we had another gang roll up on us they did a drive by on my boys house.

We were able to get down because we saw them coming down the street with their lights off, if not things would have been different. So after they shot up his house they took off, a few minutes later we could hear the police coming, we loaded the car up took off about 5 blocks away then we saw a police car and he busted a U-turn. We took a left on the next block, pulled over and we all ran, yes, we just left the car there, after hiding for about 30 minutes a few of us came back to the car and rolled out, that was the end of that night, we had many more nights like this one.

Thinking back on how many times I was shot at and not one bullet ever hit me. In one year, I was shot at 12 different times, now that I am older, I truly believe an angel was looking out for me. One time I was hanging out with my boy Carlos at his grandma house, we were walking out the front door we had a hood gangster stop his car he gets out starts to shoot at Carlos and I, we ran as fast as we could to the side of his grandmother's house to get away from the bullets. Another time I went with my sister's boyfriend to back him up with some gangster at his work, we get there and it's dark, we are in a parking lot waiting for them to come out then as they come out, we start to say what's up. I then step up to this guy getting ready to hit him with a pipe, he then pulls a gun out and puts it to my head, he then started to tell me what's up, telling me what am I going to do now.

I was scared, I knew I did not have a gun even if I did, he had his gun right at my face. I started to back up, I then turned around, started to walk towards my friend's car, as I was walking to the car this guy is still yelling at me saying what you going to do, as I kept walking to the car I see my friend Mario hiding behind the dumpster. I am looking at him shaking my head telling him no don't do anything, I keep walking to the car then this guy shoots the gun right by my ear I was able to see the bullets hit the blacktop, at this point I am freaking out, he then does it again, and I see the bullets ricocheted off the blacktop. I get to the car I turned around the guy says out loud "fuck it', he takes a shot right at me then his gun jammed.

I was shocked, he turned around ran to his car and took off, we wanted to chase him but we could hear the police coming so we needed to get out of that neighborhood. I can say that after that night I was able to step out of my invisible box of always trying to help others with violence.

The tough guy in me was learning how to balance my toughness. I loved playing basketball it was my out, playing ball took me away from all my issues, at this time of my life I did not realize all the invisible boxes I had been carrying around. I would get into fights or arguments playing basketball, it did not matter what gym, park or even at the Boys Club, I was always throwing down or being disrespectful. I have so many other crazy situations that kept me going in the wrong direction, but some how in good time I started to step out of my invisible boxes.

Juvenile Hall

Boy do I remember the first time I was locked up, I was so scared and every time I was alone in my cell room I would cry, I couldn't stop thinking about my mother. I did not get into any trouble while I was locked up, what I did was I kept to myself, I kept busy by playing cards plus going to the gym to play basketball, that really helped me, and it also helped me with passing the time. Not having any control of my freedom really made it hard and being told what to do all the time was not cool either.

Let me tell you I would spend time looking out my window, I would spend a lot of my time thinking about how I was going to change my life. Now I was arrested a lot for minor violations when I was a teen, I did spend one day or maybe a few days but I always got out right away. The crazy part was that every time I got out, I would tell my friends and family that I was not going to go back, now for the Denver Juvenile detention center, I only went twice. I also went once to the Jeffco juvenile detention center. Now keeping myself busy playing sports really helped me stay out of trouble, going to the Boys Club playing for Pal baseball league it all helped me stay balanced as a youth with no parental control.

Now sitting here thinking back to when I was in and out of juvenile hall, I know for a fact that no one at the juvenile hall helped me out. They had us going to class during the week, they did not do much to help my mental status, yes they took us to play basketball in the gym sometimes or in the courtyard. There was no one at the center that was taking the time to mentor me or any other youth that was locked up.

During my stay at the Denver Juvenile Hall there was a kid that broke out when he was in the courtyard, someone had cut the wire fence then the kid got out, that was crazy they had us on lockdown.

Keep in mind that I did not change anything at this point, getting locked up as a juvenile did not do much to make me believe that I would not come back. Don't get my message wrong, I still did not like it there but I feel that there was no impactful message that came from any worker or mentor that would have been in place at the Juvenile detention center. If they don't have a system to mentor, you or guide you it will not have an impact on your life.

The Club

Boys Club was where you could find me every day, I started going to the club when I was 8 years old. My first club was Johnson Boys Club where I went to till I was 12 years old, then we moved from the North side to the West side of town. This is when I started to go to Owen Boys Club. Now here I am 12 years old, new friends', new neighborhood at the age where I started to run the streets and getting into fights.

The club was a place where all my friends were, the place where we would play sports, the place where I had some great mentors like my coach Big Jim. This man was one of the very few people that could control me that I respected, he never had anything negative to say to me but would tell me to stay out of trouble. Coach Jim is a great man, he has always been there for not only me but many of the youth from the hood. The club helped me stay out of trouble, the club helped show me the way, I got my first job at the club working the front counter keeping the club clean plus working at the warehouse. I can't say enough about the club, I know that without it I would not have learned many things about life. The club saved my life, the club was there for me and the club gave me a chance to find myself. Know one thing about the club it was home for me, a place that I could go to and not have to watch my back.

The club gave me hope, it was the place to be at.
I remember going swimming, going on field trips getting out of the hood. I got arrested out in front of the club for a warrant I had. Boy did I get into a lot of trouble at the club, I had a bad temper, I was really disrespectful to those that I did not like. One time during a basketball game I was fighting during this time, I hit a man who is now my boss. I didn't mean to hit him, he got in my way when I was trying to hit someone else, it's crazy to think back to the things I did, plus to see how much I have changed.

Back then the club would take us on trips during basketball season to compete against other teams, one year we were at Peterson Air force in Colorado Springs. We were playing another team during the game there was a player on the bench that kept saying things out loud. While I was shooting free throws, the player of the other team continued to say things to me when I was at the free throw, I finally had enough I went at him, I hit him with the ball then the entire gym got out of control and everyone started fighting.

Coach Jim grabbed me and threw me out the emergency door in the gym, at this point I was safe I was not able to do anything, so I went around the building all I can see is people running out of the gym the M.P. Military Police pulling up. After they calmed everyone down my coach Jim somehow got us out of trouble, we then came back to Denver.

After growing up at the club it was time to move on to my next chapter in my life. At this point, I was able to step out of my invisible box I started to work, I also started to work on changing my attitude. The club saved my life. Coach Jim thank you for not ever judging me but for loving me.

R.I.P. Coach

belongings in and get issued your jail clothing, that
included shoes that others have worn (nasty). You then
continued going through the process of getting to your
pod/cell. When walking through the hallways you had
to stay on one side and on the painted line on the floor, you
stayed in a single file line and then walked up some stairs.

As you get to the pod that you are staying in, it's like a different
world, the first thing you see is a desk for the correctional
officer. You see a lot of pay phones on the wall and
lots of toilets plus the showers, all in the open not cool,
you then walk into a large room with bunk beds going around
the entire room, tables in the middle and one tv on the wall.
After getting to my bed I had the top bunk bed and the view
out my window was the courtyard.

After a few days they assigned me to the kitchen where I had to
clean the pots and pans let me tell you that job was not easy.
Some of the pots were so large that I could fit inside of it. After

working hard, I got promoted to dishwasher and that job was a little better, you needed to be fast because the dishes kept coming like crazy, you had to keep feeding the machine then on the other side you would stack them up and send them off. Now that job helped with passing the time, and after doing a good job working as a dishwasher I got promoted to serving food. At this time, I told myself okay now my job is much easier, I was feeling so much better about doing my time.

Well that did not last long because in jail when one area is dominated by one race, they wanted it to stay that way. So, if you were not the same race, they did what they needed to do to get rid of you and of course this is what happened to me.

After a few days I played my part before one of the guys came to me and gave me an extra chocolate milk and of course I drank it, it was like I was at home, it was great. I felt like it was going to be all good and I let my guard down.

A few minutes later I was called out of the kitchen by one of the officers, the officer said that the inmates told him that I was stealing extra milks. I replied that I was told I could get an extra milk, he then took me back to my pod. I then was told that my good time was going to be taken away from me for stealing, I plead with the officer that it was not true and after a day they decided not take my good time away but I did have to start all over again by being demoted back to doing pots and pans. Now at this time, I was not trying to make it back to the kitchen serving food, so I worked my way back to doing dishes and stayed there till my time was done.

During our free time I would go out to the court yard or the inside gym to play basketball, now this was back when I was young, strong and much faster. I would play ball with mainly all the African American folks and I was one of few playing ball who was not black.

Let me tell you, I was balling out and started meeting new ballers who were expecting me to be on the court, I started making a name for myself. Now this did not last for long, after playing on the court for some days others started to see that I was winning on the court. It got to the point that the Latinos started to sit, stand around the court, cheering me on. The African Americans started to cheer as well and that is when it started to become extremely dangerous on the court.

You had the people on the sidelines all talking stuff to each other and then we all started to get aggressive with one another on the court. After noticing that things were getting out of control, I started to stay in during free time. Yes, I was getting a little afraid of what could happen. A few days later some of the ballers, plus officer Compton came to me and said that I had game and that I needed to come back out to play that it was cool. So, I did and started to play ball inside, everything here was cool for the rest of my stay.

Now getting visitors was not the coolest thing ever, yes your happy that your loved ones are here to see you, but the process to get to them was not fun. They would have you go into a room with other inmates, take off all your clothes so they could check you, then you would come out to visit. When you were done you went back into the small room repeated the process of taking all your clothes off so that they could check you again, it was not cool!

During the 3 months that I did time, I missed birthday parties and my daughter being born. For the rest of my life I will always have the memory of seeing my daughter for the first time while I was locked up. Finally, the day has come, I'm getting out, the process to get out took forever, but let me tell you when I got out and my beautiful wife was waiting for me, I did take a look back at that jail and I told myself that I would never be back. This was the time when I started to tell myself that I would start changing my life. Yes, this was when I was able to step out of one of my invisible boxes.

Our First Home

In 1997, is when we got our first home. It was not much, matter fact it was a beat up little house that was about 750 square feet, one bedroom, one bathroom, small kitchen and two large rooms that were used as our living room and dining area. We had a large yard and we lived next door to our grandparents.

While we were in the mix of construction as we started tearing everything apart ready to add all the new drywall to the house. During this time our son was playing in the house with a ball, he was hitting one of the wires hanging from the ceiling and grandpa Clarence was laying down on the stack of drywall while I was working in the back of the house.

I remember I started to smell smoke, it was coming from the attic, grandpa Clarence and our son went outside, I ran outside got the garden hose and got onto the roof. I started making my way into the attic into the smoke trying so hard to keep my eyes open so that I could see where I was going and also to find where the fire was, minutes later I felt someone grabs me from behind he started pulling me backwards then another person grabbed me then another until I was out of the attic. I was then on the rooftop above our bedroom with a half of dozen fireman as they sprayed the entire attic with their water hose, everything was soaked, it took us a few days to clean up the mess.

This was the way we started off our new journey at our home we just purchased, the fire did not stop us we continued to work on the house. I got a lot of help from our grandpa Clarence and my father-in law Danny. We worked hard to get the house done, we would do a different section of the house at one time so that way we could live in the house at while we were fixing it up.

I remember when we were working on the back of the house and we knocked out the entire back part. My father-in law was on the roof and the entire roof gave out on him, he fell straight through the roof and somehow was able to hold on to the boards so he would not fall through.

Between the house catching on fire and my father-in law falling through the roof it was all new to me. I never had the opportunity to fix up a house with the help of others plus the will to work hard and learn. We were able to finish the entire house in 3 years. This house was everything to my little family, we now had something that was ours and we had our grandparents next door, life was great.

Thinking back to our first home, all the parties, barbecues we had there it was a time to remember. We were able to create great memories, most importantly this home helped us get out of many of the invisible boxes that we were living with.

After the 3 years, we decided to put our home up for sale, once we sold it we choose to relocate to a new neighborhood. We moved to Montbello in East Denver where we started a new chapter in our life. The home we bought was more than 3 times the size of our last house, our kids had their own rooms, there was a large yard, and a game room for family to get together. Yes, you can say our parties got bigger and so did our barbecues.

This home allowed us to expand our family, after settling in we had our third kid, our beautiful son Gianno. Our kids Ashley, Justin and Demi loved having him, when he got older, he would run all over the place. This new home has been a continuous change for our family, we have met so many new folks in our life, people like Tre, Tony and Shawn.

This house had a cool basement with DJ equipment that Tre, Tony and Shawn would love to mess with, sometimes they would go with me to DJ weddings or parties. They would help me for the night, thinking back I truly believe they loved it. I played a mix of music from Spanish, Country, Hip Hop, R&B and Pop, to them it did not matter, they were in their happy place.

Throughout the years of them being around me, they were able to step out of their invisible box of being nervous to being involved in music and out in front of large groups. Now years later they are in their 20's and are still involved with music.

Tre creates his own beats, Tony makes his own music, Shawn lives a healthy life with his family. These young men had every reason to go the wrong way in life but instead they grew up to be great role models, they made it out of the hood alive now living their lives.

Time to Change

Time to change, this would be the time in my life that I started doing better, this is the time that I said no more, no more going to jail no more giving my money to the court system, no more being on probation, no more getting tickets, no more ever coming back to jail. Now change is not easy and it does not happen overnight, to be honest it was hard, there were plenty of arguments between my wife and I, we had our share of ups and downs throughout our journey.

Our family continued to do all they could to make sure we did not go backwards to get ourselves in trouble. That was over 20 years ago and to this day I have not been back to jail, I don't ever plan on going back. Shortly after getting out of jail my wife and I bought our first home that we worked on for about 3 years, we both worked really hard to get this house remodeled, then we sold it and moved to a larger house in a neighborhood called Montbello in Denver, Colorado.

This is when we were living big, we had made a lot of money after flipping our last house. I remember the day when the love of my life Chantel and I went to American Furniture Warehouse. We had bought so much stuff for our new house it felt like we were rich, the entire dock was full of new furniture, it was a great feeling.

I remember when we started to put our house together it was so beautiful, amazing we had done what everyone said we could not ever do. We did it, we were living the life and we did it with hard work and by not giving up on each other.

Now here we are in this big house much bigger than the one we lived in. We had so much space, our downstairs had a pool table plenty of space to dance and set up my DJ equipment. Here we started our new chapter. After stepping out of this huge invisible box that were living in it felt great to see that hard work does pays off.

Believe in yourself, you have the strength to get away from all negative stuff around you, the hardest part is you yourself might not see the negative issues that are holding you back. That invisible box is no joke, if you feel like you are not getting nowhere then you and only you have control so get going to make that change.

Coach Age 30

Wow!! I remember when I was given the chance to volunteer at the Denver Broncos Boys & Girls Club. I was so happy, it felt like I was at the club every day, I would do everything I could to try to fit in, getting to know all the kiddos was the best part of the job.

Today after 15 years, many of the youth that I was able to mentor are now grown up. Some of them are at the age I was when I started volunteering at 30, they still come to me for advice, it's crazy to think that they are at the same age I was when I started to volunteer at the Broncos Boys & Girls Club. It is truly a blessing and all the years of volunteering all the kiddos have become family. Here I coached football, basketball, soccer, softball and baseball for about 4 years. Coaching all these sports helped me build relationships that have lasted for over 15 years, I will always remember where it all started. Having the chance to mentor youth plus see that they truly believe in you is priceless. I can truly say that

I have never cheated our youth, I have always been true to every kid that I have coached. See for me its never been about winning, it has been about something bigger. It is about change, about teaching life skills, getting out of that invisible box that many are stuck in, it is about learning to understand that all losses or mistakes are a gift, that they will make you stronger.

That has helped me grow into the great leader and mentor that I have become. I know one thing about our youth they are the future, they know so much and as leaders, coaches, mentors we need to be ready at all times to listen, to pay attention because the answers we seek are right in front of us.

Coaching has helped me guide hundreds of youth out of their invisible boxes, I have seen them take off and be successful in life. Remember we all have plenty of invisible boxes that we carry with us. Now we have to take positive steps to get out of them.

"Every child deserves a champion, an adult who will never give up on them, who understands the power of connection."

-Rita Pierson

"I may not be the one that changes the world, but I will do all I can to spark the mind of the person that will."

-Pitbull

The Wait

Playing slug bug with my daughter on the highway, not paying attention to how fast I was going turned into me getting pulled over by a motorcycle policeman. After speaking to him and finding out that I was in fact able to get my license. He was very nice and told me what I needed to do. After 14 years at the age of 30, I finally went to take the drivers test and got my driver's license.

After thinking back to when I was 16 and waiting till I was 30 blows my mind, the fact that I was able to drive that long without my drivers license. This show you that anyone can get stuck in their own invisible boxes for a long time, I got used to being that way so I chose to live that way. For many years, I spent every day looking out for cops, I would wake up day after day go to work, come home, and go the rec center to play ball.

I would drive everywhere like it was nothing, at this point of my life I just got used to driving without my license. I did not even think about having my license, I just drove. Yes, time went by as life was moving fast, and I got older I started to want to change my life. When I got out of the county jail for not having car insurance and no license, this is when I started to set a plan on how I was going to step out of my invisible box.

Now when I look back, I wish I would have done things differently like getting my license when I was 16 like most teens, being able to drive around without always having to look out for the cops. I guess you can say everything happens for a reason, maybe this reason kept me in check because I was always driving looking over my shoulder wondering if today was going to be the day I get pulled over.

It took one day playing a game of slug bug, and an officer that gave me a chance to finally step out of that invisible box that only I could see. I was able to get my license shortly after that, not to long after I was hired at the Boys & Girls Club. Now 15 years later I still have my license plus a great driving record.

"I have always believed that the best way to connect
with people is to open up, to tell my story
and expose my past."

Growing up without my Father

I grew up never meeting my father. I have always been curious to know what my father looks like and how similar we are to each other. All my life till I was about 12 years old I thought that the man I was calling dad was my biological father, after my mother and my stepdad separated this is when I found out that he was not my biological father.

So, at this point of my life I was not trying to find my father I was just living in that invisible box, I kept this boxed in for years. Every once in a while, my family members who knew my father would come and tell me that I look a lot like him, they would tell me how nice he is. It was nice to hear all this but in my mind, I would wonder why he has not come looking for me? So, I continued to live in my invisible box throughout my teen years, I was not ready to step outside of that situation.

Not having that male figure was really hard at first. Then I met Coach Jim, my father-in law who at the time was just Danny because I was not dating his daughter yet. Then my mother met Fabian who is now her husband of many years and like a father to me. So, I am going to talk about what each one of these men did to help me step out of many of my invisible boxes throughout life.

Coach Jim, thank you for being patient with me and believing that I had a future and not judging me for how I acted. Now that I am an adult he would come to the club and visit me, we would sit and talk for about an hour, he couldn't stay long because his health was not the greatest. Man do I miss having our conversations, in 2017 Coach Jim passed away.

Without him in my life I don't know what I would have done, he impacted so many young folks in his community.
Thanks Coach Jim!

When I meet this next man that helped me throughout my young days, I can say I did not like him too much. I really was not around him that much at first because I was always gone doing something, as I got older I decided to stop going to school so I started to work with him and it was horrible. It was so hard my hands would hurt, I was getting blisters all the time and I had to work 6 days a week sometimes all week, we would leave every day at about 5 am in the morning when it was still dark and we would get home at about 7 pm or later when it was dark.

Let me tell you after working with him for so many years I learned to accept him. I am so lucky that Fabian believed in me and helped me step out of my invisible box, this man taught me so much in life that to this day I still learn from him. Thank you, Fabian, for teaching me that anything is possible.

This next man has been giving me advice for almost my entire life, I knew him before I started to date his daughter who is now my wife of 27 years. Back in the day he would always somehow be around us we would always listen to him and look up to him, at the club or on the street where ever we would see him, he was always taking care of us. I remember when he would let us grab on to the bumper of his blazer and he would pull us when it was snowing, we would hang on for as long as we could, it was so much fun. As time went by, I started to date his daughter the woman that I now love so much, but during our young days we fought all the time and Danny was always there to help us. We were in this invisible box for years and Danny did not ever judge me or take sides, till this day I have never disrespected this man and I will never disrespect him. After years of being there for his daughter and I we started to step out of our invisible boxes that we were in.

If you know this man you know exactly what I am saying he is the best man, I could ever ask for he has always been by my side and by the side of many others. Thank you, Danny, I love you more than you will ever know. You have helped so many folks step out of there invisible box that I truly believe some of them till this day don't even know.

75

After years I have tried a few times to find my father to and nothing still. I have not had any luck, I really want to find him to learn more about his side of the family so that one day my kids if they ever ask me about their grandfather and his family I can come up with an answer for them.

If I ever get the opportunity to meet my father, I will have countless of questions for him. One would be why did you not come looking for me. Growing up without a father made me an incomplete person, when I was younger I never had a male figure there for me during my sports events to cheer me on, to critique my work and push me to do better. I never had that father figure there for me when I needed questions answered about what it took to be a young boy.

Growing up fatherless was very painful however I did have a few males that were there to help guide me. Many of my friends have fathers and their fathers sometimes played the role to be there for me. Yes growing up fatherless allowed me to seek out father figures that I wanted to have, like Big Jim, Danny and

Fabian. Not having a father forced me to promise myself that if I ever have children, I would do everything in my power to be a good role model, to be there for them, to provide for them, and to never abandon them.

Not having a father gave me the strength to always seek out guidance from surrogate parents, people whom I could rely on to support me in my struggles. With the support I got from those that were there for me helped me step out of some of my invisible boxes.

After living in Denver for most of my life I was able to return back to Puerto Rico after 34 years. First, I went back with my wife and we were able to spend about 4 days on the island, then a year later we came back to the island with our son and daughter, we had 7 days to enjoy the island and it was amazing.

Our daughter had just graduated from Colorado State University and she invited a couple of her close friends, we visited so many places during that week.

Stepping out of the invisible box of us not being able to travel had come to an end, we now plan on visiting Puerto Rico on a constant basis.

Cancer/Death

As a kid you grow up not really understanding cancer or death. I can remember being young and my mother going through different cancers, she had Cervical and Breast cancer. I don't remember much when my mom was going through Cervical cancer, I was too young. Then as an adult, I was there with my mom as my sister was too and we got to see our mother go through many different stages. One losing her hair that is one stage that I felt was the hardest, it was hard seeing my mom lose her hair, so with the help of others we were able to collect enough money to buy her a wig, we were able to find one that fit her perfect. Mom survived her cancers and is doing amazing now.

Growing up we have all been a part of losing friends and family to cancer and when it's someone you love and care about it's really hard. Thinking back to when my wife had to go through the process back in 2014 it was extremely hard. She had thyroid cancer and she had to have surgery and stay in the hospital for 3 days. The day we had to drop her off at the hospital for radiation we walked up to the room she was going to stay in, it was taped with caution tape and when we walked into the room most of the room was covered with a blue cover that she had to stay on. She could not leave the room during her stay. Walking away from the room after telling her bye, was one of the hardest things I ever had to do.

I cried as I left not knowing what my wife was just getting ready to go through. For the next three days we were only able to speak by phone. You know having to experience all this now that I think ack it did not take much to get me to step out of my invisible box of issues. This experience has helped me appreciate life and those that are surrounded by me. I continue to try so hard to be a better man and show my wife a different life, traveling more and spending as much time together as possible.

Death is another part of life that we all have to learn to balance, losing a family member or a close friend could change your life, it could cause you to go into many invisible boxes, that can cause you to be locked up in your own pain for a long time. This has happened to almost everyone, to get help to get out of the invisible boxes you will have to be patient, you will have to be strong, it's going to take support and one invisible box at a time, you will step out that box. During this time, it will help you help others. Working with youth and meeting new families all the time I have gone through some tough times.

Suicide has been something I have experienced here at the club, losing a few young folks, and a few young men to drugs, violence has had a huge impact to many of us in our club and community. Even myself dealing with all the issues that come to me daily with work I have to be able to step out of my invisible box that I carry with me, seeing all the death that comes with my job plus with my family and friends - it takes a lot.

I have learned to embrace all issues, to take the bad things in life and turn them into great memories. For example, losing a young man to drugs, someone that many of us cared about so much and we all know it's hard but if I choose to stay in that invisible box it would be hard for me to move forward.

So, what has helped me step out of my invisible box, I have created an annual award to honor his life. R.I.P. Joseph.

I am now grown I have seen plenty of deaths from the neighborhoods I have grown up in and now work in. Stay strong, have the strength to step out of your invisible boxes, work on one issue at a time, remember your choices don't just affect you they also affect your loved ones. Don't stay stuck in your invisible box get out live the life you deserve.

The Dream Job

I started to volunteer 15 years ago in 2003 at the Broncos Boys & Girls Club. I did this for about 4 years as I worked at Sam's Club and Wholefoods doing retail. I would come to the club after work and coach/mentor youth at the club. After doing this for 4 years, I was asked to apply for the Physical Education (PE) position and I did.

I stepped down from management in retail to start my new journey at the Broncos Club. After a year or so, I applied for the director position at the Shopneck Club, I was so nervous. I remember thinking back that if I got this opportunity that I would be so happy, at the same time I kept thinking to myself that this was all a joke. I am not going to get this directors position, when I was at the interview looking around and then we started, I remember I gave it all I had, I spoke from the heart.

I was real about everything I said, everything that was on my resume and when I was done I left that room thinking okay let's see what happens. After a day I get a phone call from HR, I will always remember the lady her name was Erin, she was so nice and during this phone call she is getting ready to tell me, it felt like she took a full minute to tell me but I'm sure it was just a few seconds. She tells me congratulations you have been selected as the new director for the Shopneck Club, I am now in shock I get quiet and did all I could not to start crying out loud, but I did. I cried because I knew I had made it out of the invisible box that I was stuck in for so long, I knew I was just given the opportunity of a lifetime to better my family.

Now that day I will always remember it, that day also was the second time that the Boys & Girls Club had saved my life. The first time when I was a kid, now again that I am an adult. After a day goes by again, I get a call from Erin (HR) she starts to talk, and I am thinking no please don't tell me that something went wrong, and I am not getting the Directors job. Instead she starts to ask if I would be okay taking on the position at the Cope Boys & Girls Club. I say yes, I would love that, I am so excited I tell her that I would take on any club. So, she tells me again congratulations you are the new director at the Cope Club.

My first day to my new chapter in life, I walked into the Cope Club and now over 10 years later I am still here and my family has grown from hundreds at the Broncos Club to now hundreds at the Cope Club. If you are still reading this story at this point you have figured out that the club is a huge part of my life and without the club and the kiddos that I have met I would and could not be the man, father, husband, mentor, coach, community leader and so much more, all this came to me by just walking into the front door of the clubs.

Having the best job, what does that mean we'll let me tell you about my job, being a director is like being a big brother to our kiddos here at the club. It's being a community leader, I have had the opportunity to meet plenty of famous people, I had the opportunity to share my story in front of thousands of people at an event. On top of having to speak to a thousand people when I got up there, I started to look into to the crowd then I see Elway, Manning, and Billups, yes, I was very nervous, I will always remember that day. I, plus a few others we're getting ready to share our stories.

I have been involved with the Boys & Girls Clubs of Metro Denver for over 35 years now. Starting as a member at the Johnson Branch then the Owen Branch until I was 18, then after taking some time away to start a family I returned to volunteer in 2003 where I served as one of the football and basketball coaches at the Denver Broncos Branch in Montbello.

I enjoy coaching and developing youth through sports, and the club allowed me to do just that. After a few years I was offered the position as their gym director where I served for a year. In 2009, I was given the opportunity to serve as the site director at the Cope Branch in West Denver. I have now been at Cope for over 9 years where I have built strong relationships with the community, schools and families. Is this job tough oh God yes, but it is not impossible we can do this, we're born to make a difference. How do I know that our young people have potential and the promise to change because I am one of them. I am product of the Boys & Girls Club.

I have also implemented the Bully Program at the Cope Branch that has received recognition from Cartoon Network and is being implemented at other branches. I have been recognized for my work with the club through several awards.

Some of my recognitions include:

2013-Billy Thomas Award
2015 Pillar Award- Branch Director of the Year
2015 Hispanic Leadership Award, on behalf of the NFL, Verizon and the Denver Broncos.

To all my kiddos, to all my young adults that I have mentored,
or anyone that has made it to this point of the book.
Have the strength to step out of your invisible boxes
and make the changes you deserve.

Thank you take care,

Coach Julio.

"Start the journey that's meant for you, we all have a past we all have a purpose, we all have a plan, we all have a story to tell. Your journey is your journey and my journey is my journey, but along the way we can help inspire others to help others with our stories, with our struggles and our pain, there's beauty in all of it, I just hope you understand that."

-Dflo Flores

Acknowledgments

To my Wife

They say for every great man there is a greater woman. Thank you for sticking with me for so many years, you truly are the reason I am the man that I am today, you have shown me how to care for others and most importantly you have seen us come from nothing to something living a good life. You have helped us step out of many invisible boxes, I love you for that. We have come a long way. We did it love. Love you

Danny Vigil

I want to thank you for everything you have done for me and my family, you are a huge reason that I am the man that I am today. You are like a father to me, Love you.

My Mother

Thank you for always being there for me. I love you more than you will ever know. You raised me good and helped me become a great man. Love you

My Kids

Thank you for allowing mom and I to guide you through life, we all have been stepping out of many invisible boxes and you all have made us so happy. Keep up the great work and don't forget to lead by example. Love Dad

Fabian Acosta

You really are the reason I am such a hard worker, you have taught me what it takes to be responsible and to be dedicated to everything I do, lastly you are the reason that I believe I can do anything. Love you

To all my Family

To the ones that helped my mom raise me thank you. Becky, I love you. You are a big reason on the way I was raised. I have plenty of memories of you taking care of me, you truly are like a second mother to me. Love you

Eric Siler

Thank you for always being a great mentor/friend, I have learned so much from your organization- Think like a Genius. Your program has helped me with many of my invisible boxes throughout the years

Coach Jim.

I know you are no longer with us, but I know you are reading this. Thank you for being in my life you are a great coach/mentor. Love you always R.I.P

Grandma Norma and Grandpa Clarence

Thank you for helping our family and showing us the way. Grandma Norma you helped me get out of many invisible boxes that I was stuck in, Grandpa Clarence thank you for showing me how to build a home and most importantly I miss the conversations we would have. I loved hearing your stories, I love you both so much and miss you.

Josh Ford

Thank you for allowing me in your life, I remember back when you were a teen, you could've gone a different direction in your life but instead you took the positive steps to redirect your life. Now you lead by example and many folks look up to you.

Much Love, Coach

To all the Alumni from my Broncos to my Cope Family

Thank you for allowing me to mentor you and help you step out of your invisible boxes. I have learned so much by having the chance to mentor you all. I am now able to help other kiddos that have walked through the doors of our club because you allowed me to learn from you. Remember don't ever stay stuck in your invisible box step out and live life.

Love you all, Coach.

The Boys and Girls Club & all the Staff and Volunteers

Thank you to all of those who helped guide me in my life.

Thanks for showing me love and caring for me.

Thank you for saving my life.

Rick Cope

Thank you for saving my adulthood life. You believed in me and you gave me a chance. It also gave my family a chance to live a better life. You have been a great boss and leader. Thanks for always being hard on me it only made me stronger and better.

Rich Barrows

Thank you for believing in me, you truly helped me move up as a Director at the Boys & Girls Club. You really showed me the way, you never judge me, and you helped my kids along the way. We all appreciate you.

Dr. Victor Rios

Thank you for inspiring me to write this book, after reading your book *Street Life*, it changed my life. Your book was the first book I ever read. Thanks again, for sharing your story.

Much Love

To all my Friends I grew up with

Thanks for being there when I needed y'all, this journey with all of us has changed us all. We are now the people that we have created ourselves to be, we all had many invisible boxes but hey we are still here. Don't stop, keep going live life, for every invisible box you may get caught up in make sure to get out.

For all my friends that are no longer with us

R.I.P.

To my two Editors

Thank you for your help:

Chantel Vigil and Demi Flores. Love you.

Independently published.

For Multiple Book Orders or Speaking Engagements

Please Contact:

Julioflores20@hotmail.com

SOCIAL MEDIA

Instagram: **@julioflores2499**

Facebook: **Julio Flores**

Made in United States
Troutdale, OR
10/20/2023

13890142R00056